POETIC SYMBIOSIS II

Poetic Symbiosis Two

Living with Addiction and Mental Illness

Docrobin and Matt Loat

This edition published 2021 by:
Takahe Publishing Ltd.
Registered Office:
77 Earlsdon Street, Coventry CV5 6EL

ISBN 978-1-908837-18-9

Front cover image courtesy of Pixabay
Internal images courtesy of Pixabay
Back cover image courtesy of Unsplash

TAKAHE PUBLISHING LTD.
2021

Dedicated once more to the lasting memory of Allan Peter Toft and Mark Vincent Loat. It spurred us on to continue our efforts in illustrating such complex issues for our readers, using both our own experiences and those of others for authenticity.

Acknowledgements

We would like to thank the following for their continuing support, understanding and friendship as part of our extended networks:

Yvonne, Samantha, Amber, Duncan, Diane, Lee, Fern, Harvey, Leo, Russell, Chris, Mikayla, Shannan, Jenna, Emily S, Benjamin, Mary, Anita, Hazel, Adrian, Sarah, Benita, Mark W, Terry, Agro, Mark L, Madison, Noah, KT, Harper, David C, Amanda B, Xander C, Kai C, Iain C, Kayleigh C, Emma S, Duane H, Lexi L, Oscar L, Anna B, Simon P, Kam S, Patricia C, Bob R, Ian F, Carole D, Marie M, Prince M, Emily T, Rednits, Anne B, Colin S, Emilie LJ, Steve H

CONTENTS

Introduction

Matt and the Doc are back again with a second volume! Reviews of their first were very positive and this seemed to spur them on to keep going in spite of the difficulties imposed by coronavirus and lockdown. Even though I have known them for a long time now, I have noticed positive changes in both of them. They have seemed particularly positive and robust during the pandemic, despite the isolation, being exposed to depressing news on television and the repeated predictions that the nation's mental health will go downhill. They have surprised me with their positivity and ability to collaborate remotely by phone, bouncing stuff back and forth by email and occasionally meeting very briefly with social distancing.

Yet again, they have managed to combine their different experiences and writing styles into moving poetry that captures the very essence of minds in their craziest states. There are startling images that defy any rationality, allied with elements of straightforward, direct poetry. They don't really break any rules of poetry, because there aren't any, and they do give a moving insight of their issues to so called 'normal' people. I have found their efforts very enlightening and I hope they do the same for other readers.

This time, they have included a brief section of quotations that they have put together from their many years of combined experience. Never mind the addict or mental health patient, some of these apply to the rest of us as well in terms of dealing with everyday life. It is clear that it isn't simply a question of "pick yourself up, dust yourself down and carry on". You also need to ask for help and listen to the advice you get. Significant change does take time and perseverance and there may be setbacks along the way. Maybe it sounds like normal life?

From that point of view, much of it is just sound advice for all of us, even if it does come from a pair of likeable reprobates! Mind you, they are still a bit bonkers as co-authors and friends. Like any partnership they have disagreements about what to include and how to write it but they don't actually have a fall-out. They settle it by playing rock-paper-scissors and can't even get that right straightaway. I recently watched them doing this and five times on the trot they drew a blank, producing the same symbols on each attempt. Then again, it might just show that their minds are in tune in a symbiotic way, rather than nuts?

Mary Fingal, 2021

Poetic Symbiosis II

Seeking Absolution?

I am all alone, desperate and in deep shit
Spiralled into abject chaos I don't know what to do
My mind racing like a whirlwind waiting to explode
I need help and surely this has to be worth a try

"Forgive me Father for I have sinned
This is my first confession
In my life I've lied, I've broken bonds of friendship and family
In pits of mortal abyss with binges of chronic abuse
Drugs, alcohol and violence were my norm an alchemy of destruction
I smiled at others' sorrow dancing gleefully at their pain
I've inflicted a theatre of horror upon those around me
They were my puppets here only for my entertainment
Car chases and parties to rival bacchanalian orgies in Rome
High octane adrenaline I'm a hybrid of villain and hero
A never ending cash-flow and that is all
I've made dreams come true and I've been their worst nightmare
I've been the apex and now I'm the prey
Scared and alone I run from my hunter
My feet refuge in the prints of the people I hunted
This coldness makes me brittle against the winds
I've burrowed in the mud and made shelter in trees
This is my sacrament
My body and blood at your altar
Seeking sanctuary and redemption
I don't deserve forgiveness, I doubted your existence
I held more value in my corruption
Despite this did you send salvatores into my life?
Samaritans that showed me great kindness
I don't feel alone anymore
For these and all the sins of my life I am sorry"

No quick fix there but at least I've confessed my sins
The true help I need now around me in human form

Help to look at myself and find the answer within
The hard work begins now and I must give it my all
Changing my life forever never to return to that hell

20 Twenty in Twenty 20

Like the hawk-eyed sniper perched in a bird's nest
Masked at the masquerade ball waltzing with unrest
Visually seeing perfection success grows from being afraid
Through all smoke and explosions from grenades

Like the overs played in cricket
The lapin critters playing in the thicket
A hindsight of future glee and seeds in a volley plenty
Striving through the clarity of victory in twenty twenty

Addict First Class

Your blind employ a masquerade of dysfunction
Carved from tortured and broken souls
Not trees like the horse gifted to Troy
Be they doctor, teacher parent or judge
Our vices taken secretly like rabbits in a hutch
Greatness or a different path defines the foreman of the jury
A functioning addict gets tested like Wilder by Fury
Not every addict sits on the street corner and begs
Some sip champagne, eat caviar and have hollow legs
With pillows of silk on which to lay down their heads
Their decline might be slower but the end is the same
The verdict of the jury is guilty as charged
Sickness and death are the sentence imposed

There's only one way to earn some reprieve
You need more than a few tricks up your sleeve
Sheer determination to see it through is a must
With loads of support from folk you can trust
Those with time and success under their belt
You can feel like you're wrapped up in felt
The days become easier taken one at a time
Soon adding up into weeks and then into months
Don't be complacent thinking you have it licked
Lest in the backside you find yourself kicked
Then back to square one – a lesson to be learned
Yet setbacks are normal and help to reinforce
There's no going back and enjoying that sauce

An Entente Cordiale?

Those great black clouds of depression
Thundering against my fragile brain
Showering me in fear and anxiety till I'm tharn
Tears like waterfalls stream into the lagoon all around me
That puddled elixir mirroring my failures and regrets
I scream and beg for an entente with my demons
For they are ever present and do not go away
Light breaks like beacons upon a placid sea
The fight's not over and I'm still here
I count the scars upon my flesh and reminisce
On the beauty and horror of their stories
Those were dark days but there are light days too
Yes, I'm a determined warrior and I'll never say adieu

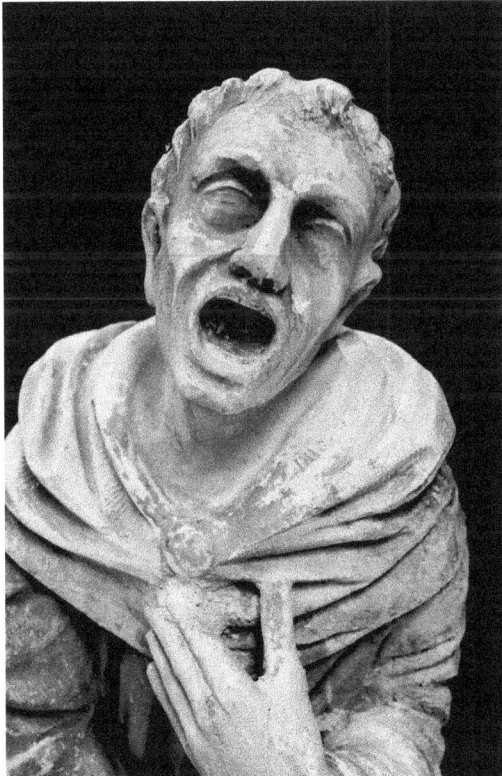

Animal Magick

I remember those nights
Like the bayou of New Orleans
Totally lost in the NetherRealm
Deep in the world of drugs and drink

That endless flow of wine and women
Lust filled bacchanalian orgies
Every desire satisfied I believed
Bathed in that juju and greed

Immortality was my fragrance
I'm the king of the quarter I thought
But nothing lasts forever
The man at the top has the furthest to fall

Hexed in the darkness, the curse broke in lux
Marinating in a theurgy of despair and regret
The alligator wizard laughed in a way that sucks
I asked was I the master or was I his pet?

Neither, I became the mouse that roared
Declaring independence from habit and master
It needed devotion with no time to be bored
Hour by hour, day by day, it couldn't be faster

Reprogramme my thoughts, leaving the darkness behind
Having faith in myself with help from mankind
Slowly but surely, it can't be bought off the shelf
Most importantly I did the majority myself

Now in a new life filled with great joy
I wish I had learned it when I was a boy
No need to look back and wallow in grief
Make the best of it and not let it be brief

Poetic Symbiosis II

To all of you who are struggling out there
Find yourselves some people who care
Then grasp that nettle and break that spell
Get rid of the voodoo and escape that hell

You might need a touch of white magic
In avoiding those outcomes so tragic
Yet find it you can if you open your mind
Then the rest of your life serenity you'll find

Bet-a Life

The deformity of ignorance is ever present in a world of pain
Beasts and birds, fish and humans too we all feel the strain
A unity with dignity seems a distant dream
In reality mankind's charity could solidify our team
We're all different but yet we're all the same
Earth as we know it is the mother to us all
The creatures who share her air, seas and land
A birthright of individuality for all of life's forms
Yet a global phenomenon of death and torture ignites insanity
The world is spinning out of control, yes it's in a spiral
I am not the only one to voice these very real fears
Heck, let's get together and make it go viral

Life is a drug and life is worth living
When the apocalypse hits and tyranny enslaves
Will you stand up for another, will you surrender
Or will you be brave and stand together
United we stand but divided we fall
Will you answer that loud battle call
Standing back to back in a wagon train circle
Facing that onslaught from every direction
Preserving freedom from oppression of all kinds
The end result a re-programming of minds
Changing lives and our future a new flag unfurls
Creating equality and a brave new world

Crutch Clutch

That thing I used as a crutch
Simply kicked me in the crotch
Left me lying flat on the deck
Physical, mental and emotional wreck

Completely ready to end it all
Made that much needed call
Future became so much brighter
Had to become a real fighter

One day at a time things turned around
No longer like a ship running aground
Now delighted to wake up every day
Dealing with life in a brand new way

Onwards and upwards the name of the game
Living life to the full like a bright burning flame
Grabbing recovery firmly with both hands
Making it clear so everyone understands

Recovery is like a breath of spring
With the wonderful stuff it will bring
A whole new life right at my fingertips
Bringing new meaning to all of my trips

Change That Habit-Hat

I've got a story to tell
About the time I crawled out of hell
Broken riddled with insomnia and debt
Outcast, seemingly forgotten by all those who loved me
Believe me how I wept
Using the kerb as my pillow
Folded down boxes as a quilt
Because my weaknesses fuelled my guilt
Thieving from everyone who gave me a second chance
Disappointments and dependence
I begged on city streets
"Any spare change"
The phrase on repeat
Dirty looks and judgement were the same on every street
Sharing needles and shoplifting
Every day the same
Running away from security guards it really was a game
The drugs you must have it
When you've got a habit
So the alley cats are fighting
Whilst prostitutes legs are dividing
Selling innocence for a fix
Left breathless scraping up coins against the wall of bricks
Just enough to buy a bag or bottle
The devil's grip around our throats
Teasing soon to throttle
I saw someone die tonight
The greedy bastard took the lot
I ran
Ran until I could run no more
So now I start to crawl
I was a whore to my addiction
There's now a choice so simple
Be the next one to die

Poetic Symbiosis II

One less fucking addict on the street
Or change my ways and make amends
Share my story
There are other survivors to greet

Daemonis et Angeli

Malevolent liquid in the glass
My grimoire of flavours rests
The rage as its strokes my throat

A festering cauldron of concoction
Mélanges of vervain and bourbon
Intoxicating it imprints my invisible walls

A hidden salvatore from the wells of misery
Apoplexies of remorse, rebirth and recognition
Myriads of questions and routes to take

To glissade the summits descent
Uncontrollable like a pinball wizard
A blind path in a lace veiled blizzard

Striking the boulder at the end of the piste
Too chaotic and filled with such danger
A simpler way sought not done in such haste

Using the slalom at a tortoise pace
Avoiding the snares and traps
A plotted route to reach the base

Do I stay put or do I move on
That journey so fresh in my mind
The touch, the taste and the smell

Am I strong enough to leave it behind?
Not back into that maelstrom of chaos
Am I the demons I so badly fear?

Poetic Symbiosis II

I must be for I lust the drink
Like a vampire lusts for blood
A mortality statistic if I re-run that race

So the answer to that question of fear is yes
Yet salvation should come from within
I must plan that journey with utmost prowess

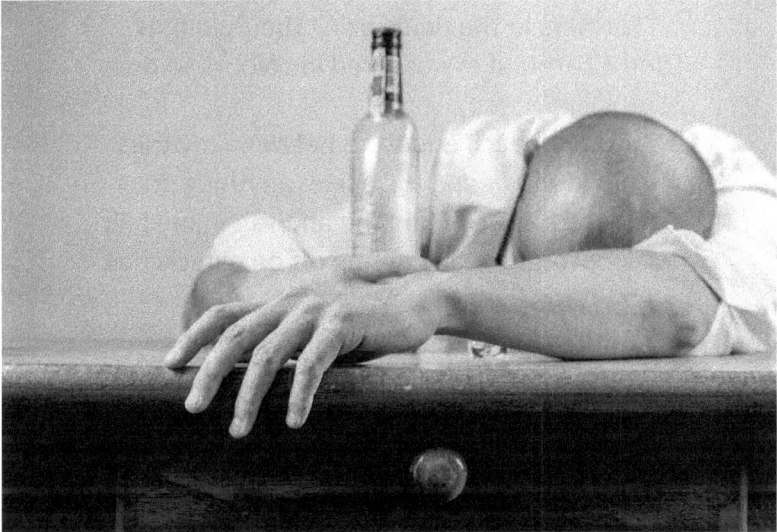

Daydream Believer

Asleep and dreaming of the long promised land
Sweeping hills, blue seas and beaches of sand
Lovely green meadows and beautiful flowery dells
An end to the misery and nights in police cells

Strolling on the hillsides saying hello to the sheep
Down to the meadows to see grazing cows
Farmers in the fields using their ploughs
Land all around me covered in colours so deep

Onto the beach and sand between my toes
A dip in the deep blue ocean anything goes
Seaweed hanging from me and salt in my hair
Back onto the beach drying off on a deckchair

Ice cream and coffee at the beachside café
A leisurely fag even using the provided ashtray
Then back to the beach to use a sun lounger
For an afternoon snooze away from that scrounger

Finally I wake up and realise it wasn't a dream
All that time that wasn't only a misty haze
That life that I hankered in those terrible days
Now my reality like the cat that got the cream

Diagnosis

Diagnosis, what is a diagnosis
Is it a label or is it a curse
No matter what it is things could be worse
The sun still rises and sets
So why should a word make us sad and detest
Maybe you cry a lot or you get angry or scared
Remember somewhere out there you have someone who cares
People may not understand you
Or what it is you tell them
This doesn't mean you're evil or strange
Simply it says to all
That we are all unique individuals
There's no such thing as the norm
We are all different in our own special way
So why do we hang on to what a textbook word may say
Diagnosis, oh diagnosis, what a silly word
If you let that control you
Then pray to become as free as a bird
Words can be strong and hurtful
Harsh and full of hate
They can also be supportive
Graceful and full of warmth
So don't let your diagnosis rule your life
Just smile as you walk down the street
Remember it is just a word

Door to Nowhere

That red face with broken boards
No handle, no knocker
Shattered splinters where the keyhole should be
It's just a door open it
Screamed those angry people who share the space in my head
I pushed against the rotten wood but they didn't give
Charging hard into the vertical barrier in front of me
It's just a door
Hours and hours with hundreds of attempts
I barely made a dent
No tools
Frustrated tears and I wailed
I need the fucking key
Nothing I did worked
You're useless it's a door
OPEN IT
I'm trapped in this invisible corridor
The damn red door blocking my advance
A feral emptiness denies me any retreat
The lighted discus was starting to dim
Fists beating into the timber
Kicks that could rival Jean Claude Van Damme
They sounded like bullets on a trash can lid
Rat-a-tat tat
My guns were empty now
The lodgers just laugh at me
It's just a door
Dropping hard to a knee
I was fucking defeated
Staring at the now all but dead light I made my final peace
This derelict corridor was now my home
Time to get comfortable
No one last try I owe myself one last try
I close my eyes

Poetic Symbiosis II

Deep breaths filling my lungs with one final charge
Suddenly one of the many squatters' voices whispered to me
I do not know who or what you will find beyond the red door
Goosebumps took over
But you cannot open it alone
A friendly tone on every word
I believed that together I'd finally be able to open the door
Three deep steps back a bullish snort
I tore through the feralness
Like I was fired from a canon
Then the echo of thunder clapped as I hit the door
A kaleidoscope of spiralling colours
Vibrant laser shows on a rollercoaster
Then thrashing against white water rapids
My feet capsized from under me
Gravity and the viciousness of the weight of the cold water
Pulled me under
Now I was drowning
I fought against the current
Threshing to find the surface
I find my bearings
Shuddering and afraid
Nothing
I opened the red door
Awake and aware
Not knowing what to expect

Entoptic Visions

Entering my mind my eyes are closed
It's just like going down the rabbit hole
The lunacy, the colours, the explosions of creativity and weirdness
Greetings from Mad Hatters and March Hares
The greying alligator wizard practicing his magic
The red eyes of the bats as the swarm like a cloud into the purple
skies
A quintet of crustacean orchestras
Feral activity in every shadow
Vampires and virgins dancing as the loups-garous harmonize their
howls
Faes of dust and diamonds chorus
Fireflies lantern the very night's coldness
Stars falling into baskets in the bayou
So what do you see when you close your eyes?

Eulogies, Curses and Omens

I've seen the effects of drugs and alcohol first hand, its destruction and
its inviting elixir. From the rainbow colours of MD2020 and my father's
Special Brew to utopian heroin and ecstasy. A concoction of liquid
voodoo that cursed and injected its venom deep into our very core.
The overdoses and violence companions in that devil's dance. I fear
that one day I'll succumb to this exocet of darkness and isolation, my
blood will carry the infectious imperfection of my kin. I'll be the one
trainspotting and intoxicated, clutching to my paradise in the brown
paper bag. One day I'll become them and bed down on the pillowed
curbs of my fore-brethren. One day will the demons win?

Free at Last?

Beware that few months-in euphoria
It is certainly not your Excelsis Gloria
Slowly, slowly the name of the game
To get rid of the guilt, pain and shame

There's no such thing as an instant fix
Take your time lest you get knocked for six
Developing more freedom as months go by
The sense of emancipation gives a new high

That darkness lightens like a new dawn
Not as fast as our fine summer days
Nor as watching the growth of your lawn
More like seasons as out the window you gaze

From darkest cold winter followed by spring
Into high summer, what joy it does bring
Real appreciation of the beauty around
Really no need to go back underground

Don't be complacent thinking you have it licked
Or else in the groin once more you'll be kicked
You just have to stick with it each and every day
For the rest of your life it becomes your new way

With that new life come lots of new joys
No more of "those" nights out with the boys
No nights in the cells or streets that you roam
Remember what happened and how you got home

What a wonderful world greets you each day
Surely this helps your commitment not sway
Then finally, at last you can proudly say
That hard earned freedom is here to stay

Fables

Staring in that empty space
Where that smooth fluid sways
Over diamonds of ice
Ferocious like a tidal wave of fire

Tracing back that trail of destruction and guilt
Live theatre I see the horror
My hands cup my head like a poisoned bandana
It couldn't be me it was my doppelgänger

No memory of the words and actions
Ma bête noire reeks of satisfaction
That glass echoes my thirst
Banshees scream "It's your round" of course

Sycophants that enable and smile at my pain
The bourbon drums beat the blood in veins
Lyrics in the fluidity, dryness in the cask
I see the lycée taught me to hide behind my mask

Disfabled

It was me that thought and did those crazy things
My mind was short-circuited and scrambled
Making me believe I was the king of kings
A life built on fantasy leaving me totally mangled

My brain needs rewiring with diversions set in place
New short-circuits to help me do the next right thing
Nobody can do that for me, it's up to me to face
Yes, I need assistance and great success it can bring

The mind so complex no human can ever understand
Yet we can re-programme it using various methods
They have no need to be clever, mysterious or grand
Straightforward is best and, if needs be, turn to your gods

Just keep it simple and safe to get the best result
Leave that old complex mind behind – it's at fault
Accept that your actions arise from you alone
Grasp your recovery and be like a dog with a bone

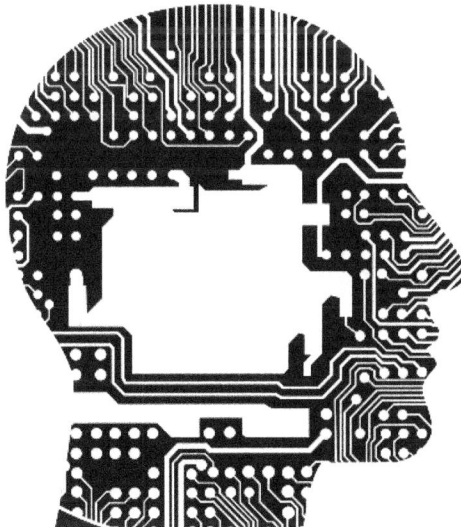

Schizotwin

I've gone all or nothing
The vault's finally empty
There's nothing left to steal
No more bargaining the hock
Just a box of dried up paints
That no one wants
Chocolate bars and sunsets
Mirrored underneath the opera house
Years of tracks and dry tears
Desperate pleas for charity
My master chemist is in his slumber
My daredevil boyfriend days
They're cold like the blueness of our abused veins
We lost everything but each other
And that brown paper bag
Thomas sleeps
But I was never awake

Follow The Cartomancy?

The haze from the street lights
Accompanying my haste
Finally the car is loaded
My last glance at the door
Now the road calls to me
The bourbon vision descends
Let's see if the tarot predictions
Are waiting for me at the end
OK my life's in a total bloody mess
Got myself in it, no more no less
The luck of those cards is no way out
A flexible plan the best way to begin
Then gotta hang on in like Gunga Din

Happy Endings

Waking each morning happy to be alive
It's time to give recovery a high five
Remembering yesterday with clarity
Knowing I wasn't a source of hilarity

No more guilt trips wondering why
I upset the world and made people cry
Accepting responsibility for myself
That can't just be bought off the shelf

No more lies to cover induced amnesia
A structured plan for the new day ahead
As time went by this became much easier
Still feeling good when it's time for bed

The journey to get there easy and hard
What you need to do so simple to see
Actually doing it is the really tough part
Achieve it and, hell, do you feel free

Dogged stubbornness kept you in chaos
Stubborn doggedness will help you escape
Grasp recovery and wear it like a cape
Wrap it around you and make it your boss

The transformation breaks all that strife
Your next tough step is to keep it for life
Just take the days easy and one at a time
Then forever you can stay out of that grime

Home Street Home

People end up homeless for so many reasons
Maybe alcoholics and addicts who didn't pay rent
Or mental health patients who don't want to feel pent
Often they're out there through all four seasons
Feeling abandoned and always at risk
Living on the streets or in tents at best
Much of society thinks they are simply a pest
Sleeping under the stars and clouds
Maybe propped upright in a phone box
So many end up wearing white shrouds
Simply treated as if they died from the pox
Getting rehomed not as simple as you might think
Many processes quite simply just stink
Hostels only provide short-term shelter
Surrounded by others with lives equally chaotic
It's just like sliding down a helter-skelter
So little support it makes you feel sick
Not the staff's fault they're overloaded
They can't be condemned for doing their best
For so many clients with so many needs
They can't afford rents in the private sector
Strapped charities, councils and housing associations
Simply a disgrace in one of the wealthiest nations
No national policy to help those in need
Not really an attempt to just plant a seed
Central government has so many questions to answer
These hapless souls are just left to wander
From city to city and town to town
To find a safe place to put their heads down

I woke Up Today II

Why I woke up today
To birdsong and sunshine
Had my meds and washed my face
Looked out the window and smiled
I woke up today

Why? II

Why did I wake up this morning?
Sober and no hangover
Greeted by my cat and dog
A brand new day with plans
Good supportive friends to meet
I love my new life in sobriety
That's why I woke up this morning!

Quis Est In Culpa?

Is this my mea culpa?
Every wrong that I cannot make right
Greeted by silence rather than words
Guilt laden twinned with remorse and sorrow
The beast is beautiful
My sweet custodian
Heartbroken by this friend
An eternal apology from me
Forgiveness never forthcoming
Just that noose of emptiness
Will it ever come to an end?

What if it wasn't my fault?
I'm not the one to blame
Why should I self-flagellate?
It was the other one who got it wrong
Maybe through actions or words
They seem to be away with the birds
Making bad choices time after time
Shitting on everyone and passing the blame
So I am not the one who is culpable
Having no need to beat myself up
Simply an honest plea of "not guilty"

Jeux de Bar Ivres

I used to drown myself in Cognac
At my broken abode or the local bar
Pinballed in traffic
Falling down in drunken Jenga
Playing twister as I scramble to the sequence of the lights
The sweetest sounds trickle like kisses in my ears
I sway and lean into the vestibule
Fingers dance across the piano
Light conversation and soft aweness
Fragrances of surrounding dew
I feel a lonely happiness in this peace
Here at the tavernes à Manosque

Écoute moi mon ami, I have been watching
You have dodged traffic and fallen down drunk
Yet you say you are at peace at the tavernes
You are deluded my friend, deceived by the poison
Carry on and if lucky you'll end up in heaven
More likely is a slow descent into hell
Recognise your illness and try to get well
There's help out there you just have to ask
Surely it's not too monumental a task
You can find a way that suits you best
There's more than one way to turn it around
Find the right mix and you too can pass the test

Judge Ye Not

Your blind and inexplicable joy
Just a masquerade of dysfunction
Carved from choices made at each junction
Not trees like the horse gifted to Troy

Doctor, teacher, parent or judge
Our vices taken secretly, refusing to budge
Something different defines the foreman of the jury
The functioning addict is tested like Wilder by Fury

Not every addict sits on the corner and begs
With brown paper bag nestled between their legs
Some sip champagne and may eat caviar
With a silk pillow to rest an elbow on the bar

Just a Shot

Just a shot of bourbon to help me sleep
Just a shot of heroin to escape reality's keep
Just a shot like swanning in the deep
Just a shot made my family weep
It took just a shot to sow the actions I reap

Validity Clock

When did I become a child of insanity
With binges and episodes denying my humanity
Twelves steps or going solo may give some clarity
In many dens sleeping in that aroma of fear and pity
Is this my first day or just a three sixty

EFF-It-Off

Sat in the corner at a lonely table
Is a man spreading his fable
Of a time when all was on fire and unstable
Sparks ignite and fly as he finally joined the cables
No longer a slave the transition totally ineffable

One-Way

Life is just like a one-way street
A short one if my maker I wish to meet
So these demons I have to defeat
To get myself back on my feet
Not covered with a white sheet

Mind Game

At last I've made up my mind
To myself to be good and kind
Leaving all that crap behind
It will be one hell of a grind
Yet what great freedom I'll find

Aurora Borealis?

Achieving sobriety warrants celebration
A unique Mardi Gras of costumes and colours
Explosive with fireworks and song
Or placid reading under a lumière contently at home
Either way the journey is yours and yours alone

Pet Therapy

Coming home to your loyal friendly pet
Nothing could be more welcoming you bet
That greeting they've given since you first met
The joy that they bring you can never forget
Keeping you sane like a strong safety net

New Days

All that effort has been so worthwhile
Retiring each night with a well-earned smile
Waking next morning with no taste of bile
Knowing the daytime won't cost you a pile
With no more sins recorded in your police file

Happy Days

Sat quietly on the sofa rolling a fag
So much better than slurping the grog
Only to throw it up into a bag
Watching the telly isn't such a drag
Another day sober and no-one can nag

Damp Days

Trapped indoors on a wet and windy day
Far better than the sunny ones back in the fray
My four-legged friends by my side they stay
Loyal companions I have no need to stray
I know that if I do with my life I will pay

Living Now

We look at our past with regret
To forgive but never forget
So full of sadness and sorrow
There could be no tomorrow

The bit in between was **today**
Knowing that now, we're okay
Just focus on that
And don't be a twat

Yesterday is history
Tomorrow a mystery
Stay in the now
You'll find a way how

Each day when it's over
Go to sleep clean and sober
A dead simple rule
But not to a fool

Rigorously applied
You won't be denied
There's a new you in waiting
It's there for the taking

Then life is a joy
For each girl and boy
Like being reborn
But a little bit worn

The new you unfurled
You can take on the world
And live life to the full
It won't be that dull

Maledixi

Both mental illness and addiction lead to lament
Each associated with their unique malediction
When what we want really is emancipation
An oxymoron with which we need to be patient

That curse will lead us once more into the fray
Haunting us daily trying to fill us with fear
60 minutes an hour and 24 hours a day
7 days a week and 52 weeks of the year

Always surrounding us by 360 degrees
From any direction it strikes us with ease
To keep it at bay we must be always aware
Or else it will give us one hell of a scare

That wake-up call is simply a call to arms
To kick it in touch with immediate effect
Delay in doing so probably our worst defect
Then it can create such multiple harms

Emancipation comes through remaining alert
Often simple guidelines are all that we need
Doing the next right thing a good rule to heed
Keeping it in the day helps prevent any hurt

Mystery in Recovery?

The art of recovery is total transition
With acceptance and an internal juju
From a loup-garou in the addict's pack
To reformed Homo sapiens lost in limbo
The bane of those guilty memories
An album of foul scented defeats
New footprints will lead to new pasture
Escape and never those actions repeat

Footprints are left one step at a time
Left with such steady determination
Walk, don't run if you wish to succeed
Take few glances behind, don't stare
Make that path longer and longer
That past now seen through a hazy mist
The present where you live each new day
One eye on the future is all that you need

Bask in the absence of the chaos gone by
Don't take it for granted keep one eye on the ball
A sense of freedom is what it all brings
Released from the shackles and into fresh air
Emancipated from that bonded slavery of old
Life now mapped with fabled paving of gold
Your head held high and shoulders up straight
The future determined by what you do next

Out of the Shadows

I'm so thankful those manic days seem to be over
It's not exactly like I'm now living in clover
Yet those wild and crazy nightmares have gone
So vivid and fearful it seemed life was done
You've probably heard about them from others as well
Rest assured, many have shared these journeys in hell
So dreadful a time that I lost the lot
Career, family, home and friends all gone west
Finally admitting that I had lost the plot
Maybe this is the time for me to do my best
I've tried so hard many times before
Each time ending up flat on the floor
Going cold turkey was simply a joke
Rattling like hell my skin would just soak
The Twelve Steps did nothing for me
Surrendering my will to something I can't see
Surely the problem just lies in my head
The psychotherapist couldn't put it to bed
Nothing but failure my head in a spin
It seemed as if there was no way to win
By chance I encountered cognitive-behavioural stuff
Not so analytical it gave me solid strategies and tips
So many simple ways to avoid those hazards and trips
Maybe this is a good way to get out of the rough
Just as important it introduced me to others
Who'd had the same struggles and had now had enough
Very soon they became like my sisters and brothers
Openly sharing their experience and knowledge
Getting to know them was such a great privilege
The support that they give can't be measured at all
By hell they stopped me from having many a fall
In a group, one to one or over the phone
It simply makes me realise I'm not all alone
Shared experience is the most valuable tool

Poetic Symbiosis II

For both the newcomer and those long in the tooth
At least so far I haven't been such a crazy fool
Simply taking life just one day at a time
Reminding myself daily to just toe the line
My new writing style shows the changes I've made
Escaping that chaos I thought was just mine
A return to that old life was simply forbade
This doesn't mean I can rest on my laurels
I still have to avoid those internal quarrels
All I can say to those still trapped in the chaos
Just keep plodding on and become your own boss

Parental Attribution

I loved you from the moment you were born
You were my pride, my joy and my heir
So soon you showed your true colours
Selfish and arrogant in the extreme
Quickly destroying my oldest dream
Behaviour erratic just like a mad dog
Out of control I was out of my depth
Not knowing what to do I did what I could
Ruling with an iron rod just like my dad
At the time it didn't seem wrong
Trying to teach the right way to be
Those Victorian values did me no harm
They made me the man that I am today
Yet now as I reflect I see I was wrong
Not knowing those generational effects
Now I can see you are just a mini-me
It's time to break that chain of inherited wrong
So sorry for my errors I hope you forgive
So we can both change and join the human race

Recovery War

At long last you're out of the rough
Why the bloody hell was it so tough
So much more to gain than to lose
Yet why so fucking hard to choose

It seems the hardest part has been done
Beware you can't think you have won
Sobriety a long war not simply a fight
Just go to bed sober each and every night

Next morning you wake without any shame
Putting it simply it's the name of the game
Life so much better with passage of time
Nothing you do need involve any crime

Your future becomes so much brighter
As long as you persist at being a fighter
You'll welcome the dawn of each day
Just so long as you stay out of the fray

Running the Gauntlet

Running the gauntlet of life
Every chamber a new chapter of strife
Sobriety and staying sane, the problems stacked
Solo or in a pack, no defence, life's on the attack

Crumbled in the ruins of failure
Perseverance, no mortal surrender, we must endure
Bombardment of challenges and riddles
The answer lies in united voices and scribbles

Like a battering ram on life's door
Throughout every trial we want it more
From our knees we scramble, we stand fast and tall
With every step further into hell we show we want it all

The beauty of surviving is a makeup of tears, piss and blood
We doubted ourselves more than anyone could
Mothers of sons and fathers with daughters
Be a lion not a lamb, don't be led to slaughter

Say it Again

So many poems say the same thing
Something in your head might go ping
Repetition is a necessity
The mother of invention
Of a brand new you

Seasons

In the autumn years of life
Neither needing nor wanting any more strife
A life emptied of hope
I just couldn't cope

The leaves had all fallen
Totally broken
Stripped down to the bark
Not much of a lark

A winter in hibernation
Working at re-creation
In that there was hope
Somehow, I knew I could cope

Spring brought regeneration
No more denigration
A new life was dawning
That I'd been yearning

Now summer's in bloom
There's plenty of room
To give others some hope
They too can learn to cope

A new autumn comes next
I ain't too vexed
Life will wind down
With no sign of a frown

Waiting for that last winter
Not so much as a whimper
'Cos when life is over
I intend to be sober

Slavery Unchained

Pharaoh's curse challenges my mental state
His priceless joy my addiction at his mercy
Pyramids of hopeless back breaking torture
Really and truly I am his lowly Abeed

Whipped and beaten by uncontrollable needs
Water bottled from the Nile and roughness of the sand
An imaginary Moses our guide to the promised land
No longer a currency shackled by evil deeds

Counting my days of sobriety and stability
Each one a slave who has been saved
Life no longer set by Pharaoh's evil demands
Now more like by the commandments ten

Free and destined to rest on arable land
Not to drown in Pharaoh's rivers of control
But to plant the seeds for a new garden
So beautiful that I must call it Eden

The Bastard Child

I'm the bastard child you never wanted
Your deepest regret
I only strived to win your love
All you gave me was beatings and hate
Never good enough
The bastard child
For years I'd cry myself to sleep
Fearing the darkness and your anger
The comets of fireflies and stars
They were your personal hunting torch
I was your son
But the bastard child was the name you gave me
Showered by your heavy hands
Beaten without mercy like a voodoo drum
My blood merged with the dirt
As you exiled your emotions
Your humanity was never there
Just cigarettes and a bourbon potion
Then the bastard child
A devinette desperate for his father's love
I count the scars
Resting on the cover of my book
The bastard child
Words written in blood

The Good Life

The new life is great
Been one helluva wait
Calm, maybe serene
The best you have been

Turbulent years left behind
But there to remind
No wish to go back
Wasn't much of a craic

But life must go on
That old one is gone
Do what's right with your time
Committing no crime

Take each day as it comes
No more sitting on bums
Join in and engage
No need for a rage

Keep yourself busy
No need to go dizzy
Balance your life
Stay away from the strife

Lest we forget
What you give is what you get
Keep to that simple truth
You too can be long in the tooth

You know that it's right
So don't give up that fight
At times it is crappy
But live long and be happy

The Man Who Never Was

In recovery I am a new man
Like the one before chaos began
But not quite the same
Playing a new game

Change – the only constant there is
Left me in a bit of a tiz
Life not at all humdrum
Left me in a conundrum

No longer a loser
Not even a cruiser
Carving a new future
Without need of a suture

Life no longer a sham
Not sure who I am
Not sure what had changed
But no longer deranged

Like I was but different
Now really content
Maybe that is because
I am that man who never was

The New Life

That old life is lost
What a terrible cost
Losing the lot
It can't be forgot

Can't turn back the clock
Just be back in the dock
Don't know what's in store
Had to shut tight that door

But it made me who I am now
The best of the old can now take a bow
The old not forgotten
Some was so rotten

Onwards and upwards in a new life
New ways to deal with the strife
Not quite been reborn
Just not so forlorn

From darkness into the light
Worthy of that long, hard fight
The old life now rests in peace
I have got the golden fleece

A new group of peers
With sensitive ears
All sharing that dream
Of not chasing the scream

We do it together
If needs be forever
Not always agreeing
But no longer fleeing

The Recovery Wall

Getting into recovery is like building a wall
No sitting on top, you are destined to fall
Probably the wrong side where you will land
Hitting hard concrete rather than soft sand

Even from the right side you need to look over
Be reminded that past life wasn't lived in clover
Look but don't stare and just keep plodding on
Treading your new path, you haven't yet won

Taking your life just one day at a time
Making that wall longer but never too high
You can keep glancing over, no need to climb
Get those reminders and give a gentle sigh

No need to dwell on those cock-ups of old
Make those steps forward increasingly bold
Leaving those memories where they belong
Forgive don't forget and make yourself strong

The Revelation Room

My name is ....
And I'm an addict
My story is full of tears and heartache
It's also really funny
I remember this one time I was bombed out on LSD
Within an hour of dropping
I was dragging my family up to the roof to meet Santa Claus
They all said he wasn't but I knew he was there
He let me talk to his reindeer
Miserable bastard wouldn't let me take the sleigh for a spin
Though he did give me the gift of flight
Yep I thought I was Peter Pan
Flying away to Neverland
Granted I hit the cement slabs in our front yard and broke my ankle
but I flew
I defied gravity
For four seconds but still hey without wings I flew for four seconds
Have you ever done that?
Another time this was on Angel Dust
Ahhh, Angel Dust, the name really didn't do it justice
Those tiny crystals really made me feel like I was in heaven
Talking shop with the big cheese himself
Good times
And when I first tried ecstasy wow I fell in love
I never knew the world held so much beauty
I kissed trees and danced with wheelie bins
There was never any bad shit going on
Every moment was like a dream I never wanted to wake up from
And then I discovered heroin
Oh heroin my best and only friend
Never once did you let me down
If I had to escape reality you helped me
Relief from the pain of existence seconds after that needle left my
arm the pain was gone

Poetic Symbiosis II

Well this all sounds like a right jolly time right
I gained so much happiness from my drug use
I also lost my children
My family cast me out
I have Hepatitis C
For all the drug use and false joy I had
I lost the only thing that truly mattered
If anyone says that drugs, drink, sex or gambling makes you happy
Don't believe it
Nothing ever made me more miserable

The Torture Chamber

In my lonely chambre de chasse
Surrounded by razor blades and bourbon flames
Broken chess pieces
Grimoires of black magic and shattered texts
Vervain laced decanters
Raging against my very soul
Photographs of loved ones
Burning
Dripping oils and hot waxes into my cup
This lycée of devinettes
A place solely to jeter aux oubliettes
A mélange of l'ange blanc and la bête noire
Bonded to that anchor
This cerebral prison cell cold and shadowed
Invested solely to live alone
For my bastard status and wicked deeds
I'll never again see home

The Internal Exit

Listen for once instead of revelling in self-pity
I am the alter ego you've imprisoned for so long
That crap is all in the past and you let it fuel your fears
Reliving it condemns you to misery lasting all those years
Yet you and I co-exist in the same physical form
You suppress me but, hey, that's not the norm
We are as Yin and Yang complementing each other
To live in balance and harmony and not be in a lather
Together we really can turn that dark grim life around
Unlock that cell to set me free and get it off the ground
You can find help in many ways you only have to ask
In time you'll find you've climbed out of shit-creek
Then we can both move forward into the light you seek

Turned Out Nice

A New Year's Resolution
That's no solution
Just words, maybe spoken
And so quickly broken

If it ain't broke don't fix it
If it's working stick with it
Just more of the same
That's the name of the game

You've been round the block
You don't need a clock
No counting the days
That's life in a haze

One day at a time
You're doing just fine
Just stick with your mates
You'll close those gates

It's not overnight
But keep up the fight
Then life turns around
You're breaking new ground

There's a new direction
Beyond your expectation
Can't change your past
You're learning so fast

A new you today
Just saying hooray
A new you tomorrow
Not wallowing in sorrow

Poetic Symbiosis II

Just do the right things
Use your new wings
Be a good chap
Fly away from the crap

The gifts that it brings
Better than the three kings
You aren't a messiah
Just a damned good trier

U Turn in a Circle

Patterns of life are circles overlapped
Which one drowns me in darkness or frees from the trap
The acolytes that enable our crimes
A fable of Russian roulette, do I die this time
Every chamber loaded with a vice or condition
They've loaded the gun they're part of the problem
Desperate to kiss that needle or pull that arm
Every time you cave you're doing me more harm
Bought off, I embarrass you and disrupt the fucking quo
An alley of piss and blood you knew where I'd go

No longer a game of life versus death
The one proviso is that thinking must be changed
No matter how you do it, just stop it being deranged
Not simply a matter of "pulling yourself together"
It takes dedication to break that noose of a tether
An ongoing process that might take many years
The rewards unimaginable as you lose all those fears
That grandiose self-delusion in life at its worst
Replaced by simple joy, gratitude and being serene
Turning your life into the best it's ever been

Victoricipation

Victory, emancipation and being set free
Not quite so simple as counting to three
So many things that need to be changed
Lest we end up completely deranged

Not just in ourselves but in wider society
Getting rid of those stigmas not that easy
We must change and they should not judge
Done with sincerity and not just a fudge

With time and diligence we create a new life
Not the same as before, it takes on new form
Away from that old one of chaos and strife
A world of opportunity becomes the new norm

Embrace with both arms and stick to your guns
We are not expected to live like monks and nuns
It's amazing what can be achieved in our sobriety
Be a productive and valued member of our society

The best things in life are what we are yearning
Ongoing calm with neither pain nor craving
For that past chaos, darkness, emptiness and soul
Ever grateful for having escaped that big black hole

Waxing Lyrics

Wake up in the morning for one very good reason
No more need to reach out for that bloody poison
Greet your day with renewed hope and a smile
OK, you won't be able to break the four minute mile

Have a clear plan for the day to fill up your time
Who knows you could end up putting it in rhyme
Therapy in seeing your thoughts down in words
Challenging your mind-set with a pen not a sword

A biography of events and situations
Engraving the paper with endless incantations
Sharing a story of our ups and downs
Pivoted at the carousel of life's paupers and crowns

Worthy text on screens or notepads
Can pull us through anything be it good or bad
The rare commodity of being pleased with one's self
Starts with the kindness to admit you need help

You might ask it of others to get a kick-start
Navigating the maze can be one hell of an art
Like drawing, painting or writing things down
All therapeutic raising a smile not a frown

Withdrawal Pains

Shivering in the blueness of flames
My head is screaming
The torture of internal yearning
Save me from the withdrawal pains
The lusting for that cursed essence
Digesting the Wolfsbane and water
I burrow my shallow tomb under quilted weight
Lost in this familiar cave in hell
More like a coven of broken men

Starting on the journey was my choice
The helter-skelter decline out of my control
There must be a way out
There's no Emergency Exit sign
I cannot turn back the clock
Like Nelson at Trafalgar "I see no ships"
The enemy is invisible it must be inside me
The way out becomes much clearer
I need to change my thoughts and life

Withdrawal is a nightmare in hell
Handled with care and self-respect
Start the journey to becoming demon-free
Engage with that foe on a daily basis
Grit your teeth and carry on
Jump aboard the lifeboat if needed
It won't happen overnight
When it does you keep on rowing
Avoiding Nelson's Kismet

Toxic Thoughts?

Addicts and mental health patients
Share many a strange characteristic
Thinking that seems to make no sense
Behaviours that are far from simplistic
The causes are clearly quite different
Although management shows similarities
Final outcomes are just polar opposites
The patient may take psychotropics forever
For the addict the solution is never
Talking with peers for both is essential
Advice given as good as professional
The combinations can go on forever

B&B&B

Bourbon, bastards and bollocks
My journey throughout this enigma called life
Bar room brawls leave a turbulence in my core
Bowling for bastards with billiard balls
As the bourbon barrels are running dry
The broken jukebox of Belfast Boys
Window's exploding like Smashing Pumpkins
Bar stools and blasphemy
Lingering smoke from cigarettes
Blood soaked lips and booze vision
Barmaids and their blarney
A smiling Beelzebub in the corner
Blinking lights as the banter expands
Erin go Bragh
Welcome to Ireland

The Invisible Man

You stared straight at me
What did you first see
An overweight bald guy
With bad fashion and glasses
Immediately you judged me on my size
You didn't see the times I was sexually abused
Or the times I was fighting to survive
My own brother has tried to stab me twice
You didn't see my scars
Or my anxiety because people get too close
You only saw the man in front of you
I'm sure it never occurred to think what I have been through
Society is blessed with ignorance
Not many people will ask you what is on your mind
2020's motto was supposed to be "be kind"
Many people hide things behind their smiles
But if most of us walked their journeys we wouldn't last a mile

Cliff Diving

It's 3am again
The sweet saltiness of that coastal air
Carried in the celestial kite before me
Swaying caresses on the jagged rocks
A view in darkness of unknown beauty
That no camera or light can capture
Orcas mirrored eyes reflecting the shooting stars
My toes tease the edge with their massage
The audience of spectating takahe
"Cheehoo"
As I take my blind leap
Breaching the placid waters
Ruku Pari
Seeking the freedom from my insomnia
In the Pacific Deep

Time and Experience

Time and experience are important in recovery
Which matters most is the question we ask
All we know is that it's one hell of a task
They say it never ends and at times you get weary

As time goes by the process gets much easier
Gaining experience makes you get stronger
The two inextricably linked in a conundrum
The one sure thing is that life won't be humdrum

Time served must be allied with personal development
Without that the time served is far less important
Twenty years clean but with twat-like behaviour
Then time served has been far from your saviour

Yet, two years in with a reprogrammed head
You have moved on in great leaps and bounds
No longer pursued by those ruthless hounds
Each night you can sleep safely in your own bed

Which path you take is always your choice
Just remember there is no instant or quick fix
You must stop repeating all of those old tricks
Then you can shout "Recovery" in a loud voice

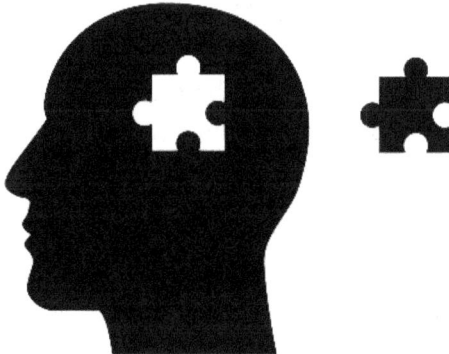

Dear Diary

Dear diary
My cycle of insomnia is back
It's 4am
The night is so silent
I hate it
Overthinking and paranoid
Waiting for my narcotic bailiffs to visit
I've hidden the hammer under my pillow
Damn it
The debts are piling up
My fear is rife
Surely the neighbours can smell it
I'm scared
No cash, no credit
Just a lottery of IOUs
Fridge is empty, freezer too
Only thing I found was an out of date pot noodle
Fuck
There's nothing left to pawn
Can't borrow or beg
I'm too anxious to leave
What if they're waiting for me
Shit was that the door
Letterbox got caught in the wind again
I'm desperate
They're coming I know they're coming
It's so cold
The urine coloured sleeping bag isn't providing much heat
It's only 18 floors between me and Kyre Street
.... can't pay .... they'll kill me ....
It's the only way

Cheque In

Checking in on the daily
Through happy times and insanity
A simple message or call
Can be the catching arms whenever we fall
Words on a screen or dripped in the ears
Problems shared help to halve our fears
A safety net from an acquaintance or friend
No matter what we all need one on whom we can depend

Nature's Tent

Laying my head down
Nestling into the white gold diamonds in the sand
A million stars across a purple sky my quilt for the night
This feeling of paradise surfs over me
A wave of utopia and peace
Lanterns of fireflies singing against nature's gentle breeze
Comfort infectious from the tranquillity of harmony rest
Life's aroma a hidden spiritual hepatitis
Release all the doubts
Cuddled into love that surrounds
Drift and dream as the rattle of the trees becomes a soothing distant
sound

My Way

Maybe my childhood hides something to blame
For my stupid behaviours later in life
Perhaps that scald at nineteen months old
From a pan of boiling potatoes
Too hot for my mother to hold
Six weeks in hospital, three in isolation
None of it remembered maybe just blocked
The permanent scar skin grafted at nine
No resentment there I just got on with life

A family not tactile maybe I didn't feel loved
We didn't do feelings, frustration or anger
Chaotic teenage years for no apparent reason
A right tearaway each and every season
Who really grew up at seventeen years old
A good education and professional career
The next two decades stable and happy
Life fell apart after death of my brother
Hot on the tail of my matrimonial treachery

Couldn't handle the pain and guilt so hit the bottle
Marriage gone west and then so had I
Two more unsuccessful partnerships
Still gripped firmly by the siblings curse
Finally broken and so close to a hearse
In that desperation just screaming for help
At long last the penny had dropped
Change my life now or be six feet down
With good support it turned round quite fast

Poetic Symbiosis II

As for the drinking I remember my last
Now where it belongs deep in the past
My final conclusions in my recovery
Don't dwell on the history I can't really recall
To be open and honest about how I feel
Most importantly I live life one day at a time
Always aware it can bite my arse out of the blue
At least now I know what it is I have to do
Keep it simple, safe and do it well

Friends are Cunts

Like the quart walking on Abbey Road
I believe my fire can do more than explode
Lyrics with a silent flow no tune or melody
But awareness of the dangers of reality
Thousands of addictions
With endless conflictions
Roads or rivers
Not all have an end
Sometimes that nagging cunt
Is just trying to be a friend

Judas of the Winter

Like the thunderstorms of November bound
The snow cold and white blanketed on the ground
Rain splashing against a man's brow and crown
His breath against the wind the only sound

Laces of fog and mist the veil before me
Scents of fresh birth among the dying trees
Unmasked from the fires adorned ravens against the stars
The seasonal Judas leaving footprints near and far

Becoming the inner demon raged in flame
Like a puppet on a string no longer know your name
Mind-fucked into madness and mayhem
Prophesied like the babe of Bethlehem

Stories of actions and word paged in purses
Hexes of voodoo and witchcraft sorcery curses
Social devastation and anxiety showered
A simple belief and man can be powered

Betrayal and treachery the common traits
They say there's love shown between mates
Not one Last Supper shared to end a life
Here in the City of Culture its curtain calls with a knife

La Route Blanche du Bonheur

You've had a hard life, that's no mystery
You blame the world for all of your misery
Much of that darkness comes from within
Chaotic thinking got you in this crazy spin

Childhood trauma might change life's direction
Influencing, not defining, your final destination
The choices you make on life's complex road
Determine the outcome and your final abode

You are the one who chose to leave home
Finally snared by the trap called addiction
Its vice-like grip has you like a dog with a bone
The inevitable end result – leaving you all alone

You've hit your rock bottom in deepest despair
Now is the time for you to turn life around
Or quite simply you'll end up underground
Please listen carefully and sit on this chair

There are many ways to get out of this mess
We can start now by getting you off the streets
Then start a recovery programme, nothing less
It'll be tough and it might take several repeats

It takes guts and determination but never lose sight
That endgame will bring phenomenal rewards
You will sleep so well each and every night
Best of all, no time in the emergency wards

70

Moxie Mayhem

When the mayhem is your moxie
Let your split take all proxy
The keys to happiness lay in the deep dark hole
But once you unlock those doors the world's your own
Scared and lonely for many a chapter
You've broken the circle and escaped capture
Mayhem was your moxie it sits in your past
Now it's the future where your days are cast

SuiCide

Do you know Sui?
Sixteen people a day say that they do
With arms wide open she'll never say no
Sui greets you with an inviting smile ready steady go
With the curtain call in the wings she waits
Ready to escort you hand in hand through the Purgatory Gates
Sweet Sui she's a charmer she takes you on a ride
Did you really want to? Please meet Miss SuiCide

Cage Elements

Your cage is like water
It can be moved and tamed
Mine is an inferno
Trapped and shadowed in flame
Both in solitary confined in a barred square
Convictions answered in Purgatory our souls laid bare
An eternal sentence no parole for the behaviour
Addict or inmate you are your only real saviour

Takiwatanga

I'm a puzzle, an enigma
I'm a mystery
Please don't treat me different
I am only being me

Lost in my own time and space
Takiwatanga for use of a single word
I'm not dangerous or evil
I just live in my own world

I mean not to be rude
When I avert my gaze
I am socially unsociable
Often in a daze

I know I'm not the only one
To some I'm merely a statistic
But throughout life's Rubik's Cube
I'm proud to be autistic

Ten Commandments of Mental Health

Mental health is real
It chooses anyone to face its ordeal
Support and medication a must
Trauma leads to difficulty to trust
Impulsive actions and pain
When in mania the cycle repeats all over again
Young or old, third or first class you'll battle
Your internal thoughts rage at full throttle
It's OK not to be OK everyday
Be true to yourself and have faith in you come what may

Tristesse Noire

Mental I have to do this
Wet palmed with fear and anxiety
You took my childhood with you
When you walked out that red door
You didn't even look back

Crying into my pillow every night
Winter winds would freeze the tears to my cheeks
I ran away to find you once
Just eight years old
Wandering the streets

You abandoned me
The drugs and bourbon were my mask
Where were you when I overdosed on heroin
Or when the paramedics thought I'd died

I'm a whore to the needle, the bottle
I've never known happiness
But you have you don't care
You left me with someone who was never there

Homeless at thirteen pregnant at fourteen
I needed you I NEEDED YOU
Surviving on paranoia and food banks
Judged by everyone I'm just a fucking junkie

Old Blue Eyes

My broken blue eyes
They tell a fable
Violence and heartbreak
Drugs, alcohol, betrayal and death
Entoptic mirrors into my soul
Like the chameleon
A kaleidoscope of colours
The core an indigenous black island
Locked by this ocean
Now the waters are running red
Lustful
Full of anger, ire and revenge
You see the devil before you
The board and pieces are in play
Erupt or evacuate
Reveille
Do you still see the beasts, red eyes burning
Or the reflection of the sun in my bayou of learning

I Will Survive

Survival isn't pretty or easy
It's fucking anxiety at 2am
Cancelling plans last minute
Avoiding everyone you care about
Months of solitude
Crying for no obvious reason
Scarred arms
A new hair colour every week
Daily medication of playlists and pills
Spending sprees on Amazon and ebay
Hours scrolling through TikTok and Instagram
Inside my head I'm screaming
But no words leave my mouth
Binges on chocolate bars and Magnums
Feeling safer with rabid animals than people
Scraps of paper with poetry and song lyrics
A tapestry of chaos and confusion
Weeks or months of insomnia
Netflix and camp-outs on the couch
Surviving isn't easy
But by fuck I survived

Happy Days

Each day is now very similar and stable
Waking each morning feeling very able
Fresh and ready for what the day brings
No more hangovers or related things

Three meals a day almost to a timetable
A flexible plan for the day, if I am able
Only interrupted by cats wanting food
Or an Old Bat in another strange mood

These can seem like a barrage at times
Screwing the plans up but what the hell
Frustration not anger and the day goes well
A calm frame of mind committing no 'crimes'

Such a contrast to those days of yore
Living in chaos totally out of control
So glad it's behind me I want it no more
Ongoing sobriety my one and only goal

These days might sound very boring to you
Believe me they're not there's plenty to do
Just keeping busy and not too long alone
I don't have to see people I do have a phone

Continued support is vital to staying on track
Helping to avoid that unexpected attack
From that enemy I thought was my friend
Now preventing that premature dead-end

Lost Daughter

I had a young daughter
Didn't care as I oughter
Not thinking quite straight
I slammed shut the gate

As drink took a hold
I lost all my gold
Chaos began to unfurl
And I lost my little girl

What taunts did she hate
At the school gate?
"Your dad's a drunk
He should do a bunk"?

That's what I did
As I went and hid
Deep in the grog
Much worse than a bog

But from that dark world
A new life unfurled
Now dry and stable
With food on the table

Hope for the future
Not needing a suture
Focused today, an eye for tomorrow
No intention to cause further sorrow

Life gets nearer its end
Can she be a friend?
Sweep aside all that hate
Before it's too late

Poetic Symbiosis II

Or will she forget
Maybe live to regret
No-one close-in to call
Should another take the fall

Hello Luv

Two words
Eight letters
Fifteen years of abandonment
Photographs in a million fragments
Many a night sleeping on a tear soaked pillow
I never forgot your name
In the evensong I prayed
For your happiness, to one day see you
I was always alone in crowded rooms
The solitude and coldness
As bad as it was, nothing hurt more
Than losing you
A broken morning
Grey clouds and an orange sunrise
Highlight the notebook on the desk
A lavender rosary breaching the pages
The distant ringing of church bells
I never thought this day would come
On the other side of these iron gates
To finally see you
My daughter
Two words
Eight letters
"Hello luv"

Poetic Symbiosis II

81

Cockney Intro

Once again, after the therapeutic process of writing a series of revealing poems, we felt the need to vent our spleens in a bit of dialogue from the crazy cockney. Having once more explored some difficult personal material over a considerable period of time we can only emphasise the value of engaging in some kind of light-hearted creativity. We have had a real laugh with this and it helps to distract from the doom and gloom so often associated with the material in the poems.

A Cockney on the Cobbles II

Listen here mush you are talking a load of pony. I heard different kid, you were proper elephants as the sun came up you Berk. Her indoors sent you to get some scran and you ran ya north at her. All because you were off the wagon. Ya were tooled up to bump a motor, you had a pouch of majestics in ya sky. Ya nowt but a fuckin tea. Plod moved you on so you went dahn the rub, not to clear ya napper but so you could get even more hammered out ya crust, ya merchant. As for ya trouble and her blister, ya tried to hit 'em both in the Hampsteads, not some aver geezer, ya pikey twat. And it wasn't er blister that kneed you, it was a local tart whose Bristols you'd grabbed. As for staggerin dahn the frog, ya wuz bein marched by the filth. You called him jinja while you wuz fondling his Khyber. No bladdy surprise ya wuz slapped in the floweries for the night. As for the Richard, he did a real solid, you should have bin doin real bird, ya prat.

Time to get back on the fackin wagon ya right royal berk.

Might see ya 'round kid.

Quotations

The following quotations are ones that we have developed through our own treatment and/or recovery. They have emerged as a result of both our own experiences and the words of wisdom we have picked up from others we have encountered on our journeys. Some may seem familiar, being variations on other people's writings or spoken words, but they have been re-expressed for the contexts of addiction and mental illness. Hopefully, they might help to motivate others to begin or stick with their own treatment and management. Perseverance is the key to success!

"Not all addicts beg on city centre streets, some are in charge of the courts, surgeries or even the country"

"Sometimes you need to burn the house down to see who will dance with you in the flames"

"Every bad day ends with the sunset and the sun rises the next day with a chance to start again"

"It is better to try and fail than not try at all, but remember to try again"

"Life is a time-limited gift, often shortened by our own choices"

"The rock star oath is sex and drugs and rock 'n' roll – the recovery oath is one day at a time and I'm not alone"

"Recovery is like a tree trunk – there are many routes on the way in and many branch roads reaching out; all of these entries and exits share the trunk

"Do not fear where the next drink may take you, relax in the knowledge of where it WILL take you"

"Not every addict's addiction or recovery journey is the same; map your own path"

"Experience cannot be measured by time alone because you can gain a lot of experience in a short time"

"The human body is gifted with two ears so we can listen twice as much as we speak"

"Addiction is something that you must learn to live with and not suffer from"

"No purpose in building a bridge if no-one wishes to cross the river"

"When they no longer need you, some 'friends' show their true colours"

"Reconciliation takes time, a precious commodity whose true value we may not realise until it is too late"

"Recovery is easier if the theory is kept simple" (based on Occam's Razor Principle)

"Judge me for who I am, not what I was"

Poetic Symbiosis II

Epilogue

La Raison d'Être

Cerebral Symbiosis?

Minds may work in many different ways
Some as apparently random vivid images
Others in logic making sense of the haze
So different they are kept in separate cages

Maybe like the arts and the sciences
There's not much common ground
Just dig deeper and tear down fences
Working together we turned it around

Two poets with styles seemingly worlds apart
One complex imagery based not relying on rhyme
The other using rhyme and direct from the start
No common ground but we gave it some time

More in our backgrounds than we first thought
Experiences and incidences that were so fraught
Both wanting a way forward and a means of escape
It wouldn't be provided by some guy with a cape

Using our own styles provided a good start
Sharing thoughts and efforts started a change
Creating a new style that's straight from the heart
Using our efforts as catharsis wasn't so strange

The bond developed like attraction of the opposite
Mutual support and understanding forming the core
Different ages and backgrounds stop it being a bore
We both wish the other would stop talking such shit

The partnership based on mutual confidence and trust
Keeps one from the asylum and the other from booze
Working together in unity makes sure we don't lose
We call it Poetic Symbiosis and it's something we lust